AN UNLIKELY LENT

LEADER GUIDE

An Unlikely Lent
Extraordinary People
of the Easter Story

An Unlikely Lent
978-1-7910-3733-8
978-1-7910-3735-2 eBook

An Unlikely Lent: DVD
978-1-7910-3737-6

An Unlikely Lent: Leader Guide
978-1-7910-3734-5
978-1-7910-3736-9 eBook

RACHEL BILLUPS

AN
UNLIKELY
LENT

EXTRAORDINARY PEOPLE OF
THE EASTER STORY

Abingdon Press | Nashville

An Unlikely Lent
Extraordinary People of the Easter Story
Leader Guide

978-1-7910-3734-5

Cover description: Background is white with a gold floral border. A crown of thorns is at the top and a small rooster at the bottom. Title reads *An Unlikely Lent* with subtitle *Extraordinary People of the Easter Story* by Rachel Billups. Purple silhouettes show a donkey, open tomb, dove, and three crosses. A purple banner at the top says Leader Guide.

MANUFACTURED IN THE UNITED STATES OF AMERICA

CONTENTS

Introduction: An Introduction to a Different Kind
of Lenten Journey 7

Session 1. Unlikely Offering: Mary of Bethany 11

Session 2. Unlikely Opposition: The Servant Girl 20

Session 3. Unlikely Freedom: Barabbas 29

Session 4. Unlikely Companionship: Simon of Cyrene 38

Session 5. Unlikely Courage: The Women at the Cross 45

Session 6. Unlikely Allies: Joseph of Arimathea and Nicodemus 53

View a complimentary session
of Rachel Billup's
An Unlikely Lent

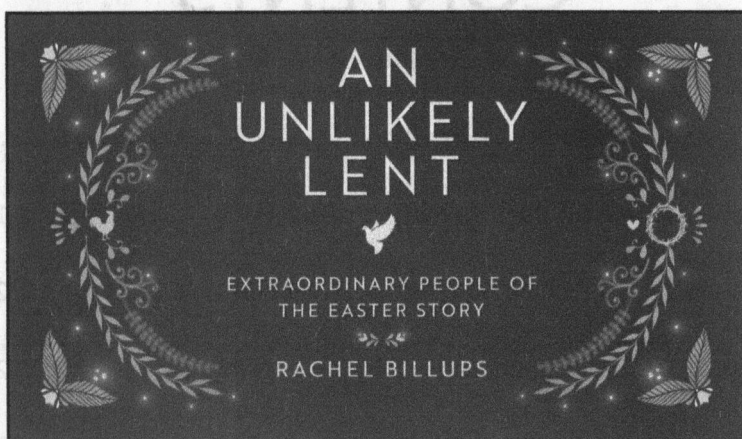

AN
UNLIKELY
LENT

EXTRAORDINARY PEOPLE OF
THE EASTER STORY

RACHEL BILLUPS

Scan the QR code below or visit
https://bit.ly/anunlikelylent.

INTRODUCTION
An Invitation to a Different Kind of Lenten Journey

The story of Easter is rightfully centered on the crucifixion and resurrection of Jesus. We speak often of the pain, the nails, the crown of thorns. We hear of the Roman soldiers and the key players, such as Pontius Pilate, Peter, and Judas. But what about everyone else? The ones watching, grieving, wondering? What about those who don't hold the central roles but whose stories still matter?

Jesus's arrest and crucifixion were not witnessed in isolation; these events unfolded before a crowd. In that crowd were women and men who slipped through the margins of our Bibles, people who stood in the shadows but whose presence still shaped the moment. People like the servant girl who confronted Peter, and Simon of Cyrene who was just minding his own business when he was compelled to carry Jesus's cross. Might their stories have something to teach us today? Might we find in them an invitation to a different kind of Lenten journey?

Introduction

This study, which is a companion to *An Unlikely Lent* by Rachel Billups, takes a close look at some of these unlikely people we encounter in the stories about Jesus's death and resurrection. It includes six sessions, each of which corresponds to a chapter in Billups's book:

+ **Session 1: Unlikely Offering**—In the home of some of Jesus's closest friends, Mary of Bethany steps forward in a bold and lavish act of divine adoration, anointing Jesus's feet with a costly perfume. Participants will explore this act that demonstrated her deep love for Jesus while foreshadowing his impending death and burial, considering whether they are prepared to defy the norms of the day and offer Jesus their unlikely offerings.

+ **Session 2: Unlikely Opposition**—As the journey continues, we encounter the servant girl whose words present Peter with an unlikely opposition, boldly claiming Peter was with Jesus. Participants will examine Peter's denial and be invited to explore their own experiences of opposition, considering that sometimes the challenges that unsettle us are the very ones that transform us.

+ **Session 3: Unlikely Freedom**—Barabbas, who was the one chosen by the crowd to be released instead of Jesus, is often painted as a villain, a man unworthy of mercy. Participants will be challenged to consider how his story is a reflection of the irresistible grace of God and whether there are parts of their own stories that still need to experience the scandalous, unearned, and unfair love of God.

+ **Session 4: Unlikely Companionship**—Simon of Cyrene was an outsider pulled into the unfolding drama of redemption, reminding us that just as Jesus did not walk the road to the cross alone, so, too, we need human help. Participants will reflect on how they respond when they are pulled into the suffering of others as they consider what it looks like to embrace interdependent faith.

+ **Session 5: Unlikely Courage**—The women at the cross, who remained by Jesus's side when others fled, demonstrated profound bravery and courage. Participants will consider that courage is not always loud or forceful but sometimes means bearing witness and refusing to abandon those in need.

+ **Session 6: Unlikely Allies**—Joseph of Arimathea and Nicodemus, men of power and privilege, risked everything to care for Jesus's body. As participants examine these men's willingness to use their influence to ensure Jesus was buried with dignity, they will consider that faithfulness often requires us to step beyond our comfort zones and align ourselves with God's purposes, even when it carries a cost.

Although this Leader Guide assumes all participants are reading *An Unlikely Lent*, its quotations from Billups's book and inclusion of key Scripture passages mean leaders with a copy of the companion book can lead the study effectively. Additionally, the accompanying DVD or streaming video from Amplify Media can supplement these session plans.

Each session contains the following elements to draw from as you plan six in-person, virtual, or hybrid sessions:

+ Session Objectives—Key learnings or takeaways for the session.
+ Biblical Foundations—Key Scripture texts for the session (taken from the New Revised Standard Version, Updated Edition).
+ Before Your Session—Tips to help you prepare for the session.
+ Starting Your Session—A question or icebreaker intended to ease participants into sharing and prepare them for discussion.
+ Opening Prayer—Use the prayer as written or let it guide you to offer a prayer in your own words.

Introduction

+ Video Presentation—A prompt to play the appropriate track on the DVD or the streaming session of *An Unlikely Lent* (running time is approximately 8–10 minutes).
+ Book Discussion Questions—You likely will not be able or want to use all the questions in every session. Pick and choose questions based on your group's interests and the Spirit's leading.
+ Optional Practice—A way to help participants apply what they have learned in their daily lives through either a symbolic or reflective practice, or both.
+ Closing Prayer—Use the prayer as written or let it guide you to offer a prayer in your own words.

Thank you for your willingness to lead this study. May it lead you and your group to a deeper appreciation and understanding of the Easter story and its unlikely characters, helping you to discover a new dimension of God's pervading love and a fresh resurrection experience for your own lives.

Session 1
UNLIKELY OFFERING
Mary of Bethany

Session Objectives

This session's reading, reflection, discussion, and prayer will help participants:

- think about how they have experienced Lent in the past and would like to experience it this year;
- consider how Mary of Bethany's anointing of Jesus demonstrates true devotion and discipleship;
- recognize Mary's act of anointing as preparing Jesus's body for burial;
- explore Jesus's revolutionary and deeply personal interaction with Mary and other women in the Gospels;
- examine the similarities and differences of various anointing stories in the Gospels and ponder scholars' theories regarding the possible melding of stories and female identities; and

• consider what their own unlikely offering to Jesus and others might be.

Biblical Foundations

Six days before the Passover Jesus came to Bethany, the home of Lazarus, whom he had raised from the dead. There they gave a dinner for him. Martha served, and Lazarus was one of those reclining with him. Mary took a pound of costly perfume made of pure nard, anointed Jesus's feet, and wiped them with her hair. The house was filled with the fragrance of the perfume. But Judas Iscariot, one of his disciples (the one who was about to betray him), said, "Why was this perfume not sold for three hundred denarii and the money given to the poor?" (He said this not because he cared about the poor but because he was a thief; he kept the common purse and used to steal what was put into it.) Jesus said, "Leave her alone. She bought it so that she might keep it for the day of my burial. You always have the poor with you, but you do not always have me."

When the great crowd of the Jews learned that he was there, they came not only because of Jesus but also to see Lazarus, whom he had raised from the dead. So the chief priests planned to put Lazarus to death as well, since it was on account of him that many of the Jews were deserting and were believing in Jesus.

John 12:1-11

Now as they went on their way, he entered a certain village where a woman named Martha welcomed him. She had a sister named Mary, who sat at Jesus's feet and listened to what he was saying. But Martha was distracted by her many tasks, so she came to him and asked, "Lord, do you not care that my sister has left me to do all the work by myself? Tell her, then, to help me." But the Lord answered her, "Martha, Martha, you are worried and distracted by many things, but few things are needed—

indeed only one. Mary has chosen the better part, which will not be taken away from her."

Luke 10:38-42

While he was at Bethany in the house of Simon the leper, as he sat at the table, a woman came with an alabaster jar of very costly ointment of nard, and she broke open the jar and poured the ointment on his head. But some were there who said to one another in anger, "Why was the ointment wasted in this way? For this ointment could have been sold for more than three hundred denarii and the money given to the poor." And they scolded her. But Jesus said, "Let her alone; why do you trouble her? She has performed a good service for me. For you always have the poor with you, and you can show kindness to them whenever you wish, but you will not always have me. She has done what she could; she has anointed my body beforehand for its burial. Truly I tell you, wherever the good news is proclaimed in the whole world, what she has done will be told in remembrance of her."

Mark 14:3-9

One of the Pharisees asked Jesus to eat with him, and when he went into the Pharisee's house he reclined to dine. And a woman in the city who was a sinner, having learned that he was eating in the Pharisee's house, brought an alabaster jar of ointment. She stood behind him at his feet, weeping, and began to bathe his feet with her tears and to dry them with her hair, kissing his feet and anointing them with the ointment.

Luke 7:36-38

Before Your Session

+ Carefully and prayerfully read this session's Biblical Foundations more than once. Note words and phrases that attract your attention and meditate on them. Write down questions you have

and consult trusted Bible commentaries for further exploration
if desired.

+ Carefully read the introduction and chapter 1 of *An Unlikely
  Lent* by Rachel Billups.

+ You will need Bibles (or screen slides prepared with Scripture
  texts if meeting online; be sure to note the translation used); a
  markerboard or chart paper and markers; paper, pens or pencils.

+ If using the DVD or streaming video, preview the session 1
  video segment.

Starting Your Session

Welcome participants as they arrive. Express why you are enthusiastic
about leading this study of *An Unlikely Lent* and invite participants to
briefly share what hopes they have for your time together over the next
six weeks.

Share:

+ Lent is a 40-day season of preparation that invites us to
  reengage with Jesus's life, his death on the cross, and ultimately
  the Resurrection of Easter.

+ During Lent, many people choose to engage in particular
  spiritual practices as a way to deepen their connection with
  God. Some give up habits that distract or block connection
  with God, while others embrace practices that are centering
  and life-giving to themselves and those around them.

Ask:

+ How have you observed the season of Lent in the past? How
  might you want to experience Lent this year? (You might write
  participants' responses on a markerboard or chart paper.)

Opening Prayer

God, thank you for this opportunity to have a different journey through Lent this year. As we join together in studying and discussing Jesus's death and resurrection through the eyes of some unlikely characters in the story—beginning with Mary of Bethany, who is an example of true devotion and discipleship—we ask you to open our hearts and minds to all that we can learn from them. Deepen our faith in Christ and our sense of Christian community. Amen.

Video Presentation

Play the first track on the DVD or the streaming session of *An Unlikely Lent*, session 1 (running time is approximately 8–10 minutes). Discuss:

+ Which statements most interested, intrigued, surprised, or confused you? Why?
+ What new insights or questions does this video segment raise for you?

Book Discussion Questions

Food Offerings

+ When and how have you demonstrated care for a friend or neighbor or someone else who lost someone they loved?
+ How are food offerings about so much more than the food? What do food offerings communicate to those receiving them? Share from your own experience of giving or receiving an offering of food in a time of need or loss.
+ In Luke 10:38-42 we find Jesus in the home of his friends Lazarus, Mary, and Martha before they are to share a meal. Can you find any clues in this story that they are good friends? As

good friends, do you think it was likely that they shared many meals together? Why or why not?

Tomorrow Is Not Promised

Invite a volunteer to read aloud John 12:1-3 and Luke 10:38-42.

+ John 12:1-3 tells us about a celebratory meal Jesus shared with his good friends. After hearing these words, now take a moment to glance back at John 11. What is the context for this celebratory meal? Why might there be a sense of urgency and tension surrounding the meal?

+ In both the Luke 10 and John 12 texts, we find Martha serving. Traditionally, these stories have been viewed as two different occasions. What are your thoughts regarding the possibility of them being the same story with a different twist or angle?

+ What does Mary do in John 12:3? What do you think motivated Mary to do such a thing? How did her actions add to the tension of the gathering?

+ What does the author tell us about the word *ēleipsen* (anointed), and how does this enhance our understanding of the scene in John 12?

Now invite someone to read aloud John 12:4-11.

+ What question did Judas ask after Mary anointed Jesus? What commentary does the author of John's Gospel add in verse 6, and what are your thoughts about why the author might have included this statement?

+ How does Jesus respond to Judas in verses 7 and 8, and what Old Testament Scripture is being echoed here? What are some possible interpretations of this exchange between Judas and Jesus?

Grace on the Menu

Tell participants that Jesus's interactions with women throughout the Gospels were revolutionary and deeply personal. As the author writes, "Grace was always on the menu when Jesus interacted with women."

+ How do we see Jesus value and dignify women in the stories of the woman at the well (John 4), the woman caught in adultery (John 8), and here in John 12 with Mary of Bethany? In what ways does Jesus offer each of these women dignity and grace?
+ Other Gospel writers include accounts of this type of anointing. Compare the similarities and differences of the stories found in Mark 14:3-9 and Luke 7:36-50.
+ The author notes that scholars have long chastised the storytellers of the early church for their tendency to meld all of its female identities together, and that it's possible John combined the stories from Mark 14 and Luke 7 so that Mary represents both women in a profound and prophetic way. What are your thoughts about this possible melding of identities?
+ Regardless of the identity of Mary in John 12, how does she emerge from the text as a passionate follower of Jesus? How does she offer us a picture of true discipleship?

The Offering

+ What do we know about the spikenard Mary used to anoint Jesus? Where was it likely from? How was it typically used? How might we describe the aroma? How much did it cost, and how much was that amount worth?
+ Have you ever experienced or witnessed an anointing? If so, how would you describe that experience? If not, how might such an experience be meaningful to you?

An Unlikely Offering

Share these words of the author: "In a world where scarcity seems to be the name of the game, abundance feels like a healing balm. Perhaps that was Jesus's point: this unlikely offering was over the top; a demonstration of the grace God was pouring over all of creation."

+ Why is it significant that God invites us to participate in offering grace? What happens when we say yes to this invitation and offer others extravagant generosity? Share from your own experience as you are comfortable.

+ What gifts do you have to offer Jesus and others? What is your unlikely offering?

+ How might our unlikely offerings take God's love into a world desperately in need of grace?

Optional Practice

Close the session by inviting participants to reflect on what their unlikely offering might be—some gift of love, devotion, or generosity that may seem unusual or unexpected but that speaks deeply to Jesus. Write the following instructions on a markerboard or chart paper ahead of time, or create a handout to distribute:

> Pause to reflect and journal in response to this question: "What is my unlikely offering?" Write about skills, resources, or acts of love that may seem small or unconventional but that could bless others.

Allow participants time to reflect and write. Then invite volunteers to share as they are comfortable. (Or you might break into small groups or pairs to share.)

An alternative or additional option would be to commit to giving your time and presence as a group. You might visit those who are lonely or hospitalized, provide a meal for a struggling family, give encouragement to people in need, or offer simple gestures of kindness. Discuss the possibilities and work together to plan a day of "unexpected offerings."

Remind participants that no offering is too small and no act of love goes unnoticed in the kingdom of God.

Closing Prayer

Gracious and generous God, thank you for receiving our unlikely offerings—those given from the heart in love. Teach us to give in faith even when we question our efforts and how they are being perceived. Open our eyes to see you in every act of love. May the gifts we offer, however ordinary or extravagant they may be, become expressions of your grace in the world. Amen.

Session 2
UNLIKELY OPPOSITION
The Servant Girl

Session Objectives

This session's reading, reflection, discussion, and prayer will help participants:

+ recognize the servant girl's pivotal role in helping us understand what's at stake in Jesus's trial;
+ understand the strong motivation of self-preservation in Peter's denial of Jesus and consider how self-preservation is evident in other biblical stories as well as our own lives;
+ explore the differences between slavery in the first-century Roman Empire and in eighteenth- and nineteenth-century America and reconsider the role the servant girl plays not only in Peter's life but also in ours; and

♦ remember that denial is not final; there is forgiveness,
   redemption, and restoration—in Peter's story and in ours.

Biblical Foundations

*They took Jesus to the high priest, and all the chief priests, the elders,
and the scribes were assembled. Peter had followed him at a distance,
right into the courtyard of the high priest, and he was sitting with the
guards, warming himself at the fire. Now the chief priests and the whole
council were looking for testimony against Jesus to put him to death, but
they found none. For many gave false testimony against him, and their
testimony did not agree. Some stood up and gave false testimony against
him, saying, "We heard him say, 'I will destroy this temple that is made
with hands, and in three days I will build another, not made with hands.'"
But even on this point their testimony did not agree. Then the high priest
stood up before them and asked Jesus, "Have you no answer? What is
it that they testify against you?" But he was silent and did not answer.
Again the high priest asked him, "Are you the Messiah, the Son of the
Blessed One?" Jesus said, "I am, and*

>   *'you will see the Son of Man*
>   *seated at the right hand of the Power'*
>   *and 'coming with the clouds of heaven.'"*

*Then the high priest tore his clothes and said, "Why do we still need
witnesses? You have heard his blasphemy! What is your decision?" All of
them condemned him as deserving death. Some began to spit on him, to
blindfold him, and to strike him, saying to him, "Prophesy!" The guards
also took him and beat him.*

*While Peter was below in the courtyard, one of the female servants of the
high priest came by. When she saw Peter warming himself, she stared at
him and said, "You also were with Jesus, the man from Nazareth." But*

he denied it, saying, "I do not know or understand what you are talking about." And he went out into the forecourt. Then the cock crowed. And the female servant, on seeing him, began again to say to the bystanders, "This man is one of them." But again he denied it. Then after a little while the bystanders again said to Peter, "Certainly you are one of them, for you are a Galilean, and you talk like one." But he began to curse, and he swore an oath, "I do not know this man you are talking about." At that moment the cock crowed for the second time. Then Peter remembered that Jesus had said to him, "Before the cock crows twice, you will deny me three times." And he broke down and wept.

Mark 14:53-72

When they had finished breakfast, Jesus said to Simon Peter, "Simon son of John, do you love me more than these?" He said to him, "Yes, Lord; you know that I love you." Jesus said to him, "Feed my lambs." A second time he said to him, "Simon son of John, do you love me?" He said to him, "Yes, Lord; you know that I love you." Jesus said to him, "Tend my sheep." He said to him the third time, "Simon son of John, do you love me?" Peter felt hurt because he said to him the third time, "Do you love me?" And he said to him, "Lord, you know everything; you know that I love you." Jesus said to him, "Feed my sheep."

John 21:15-17

Before Your Session

+ Carefully and prayerfully read this session's Biblical Foundations more than once. Note words and phrases that attract your attention and meditate on them. Write down questions you have and consult trusted Bible commentaries for further exploration if desired.
+ Carefully read chapter 2 of *An Unlikely Lent* by Rachel Billups.

- You will need Bibles (or screen slides prepared with Scripture texts if meeting online; be sure to note the translation used); a markerboard or chart paper and markers; paper, pens or pencils.
- If using the DVD or streaming video, preview the session 2 video segment.

Starting Your Session

Welcome participants and tell them that today you will be exploring how sometimes opposition can be an unlikely tool of refinement and growth in our lives, particularly in times of tension and strife. Share Rachel's story of pushing back against the idea that everyone can be included in the circle of belonging only to be reminded later of the reality that everyone belongs to God and to one another.

Share:

- Opposition often comes from the least expected places, and sometimes the people who frustrate us the most are the ones teaching us something valuable.

Ask:

- When have you found opposition to be a valuable teacher? (Invite participants to share brief responses.)

Opening Prayer

God, thank you for the opportunity today to view opposition as an unlikely tool of refinement and growth—an unlikely teacher in our lives. As we study and discuss Peter's denial and restoration, we ask you to open our hearts and minds to all that we can learn from the characters and events of the story. Deepen our faith in Christ and our sense of Christian community as we continue this Lenten journey together. Amen.

Video Presentation

Play the second track on the DVD or the streaming session of *An Unlikely Lent*, session 2 (running time is approximately 8–10 minutes). Discuss:

+ Which statements most interested, intrigued, surprised, or confused you? Why?
+ What new insights or questions does this video segment raise for you?

Book Discussion Questions

Tense Times

Set the scene by reminding participants that when Jesus was arrested, Peter drew a sword and took off the ear of the high priest's slave. Jesus stopped the violence with his words and healing action, and the disciples ran away to avoid being captured by the temple guards. Alone and abandoned, Jesus was led to stand trial before the Sanhedrin and chief priest.

Have a volunteer read aloud Mark 14:53-72.

+ Given what we know about the disciple Peter, why do you think he followed Jesus to the home of the chief priest?
+ What do you imagine Peter was thinking and feeling as he warmed himself by the fire?
+ Has fear ever caused you to hold back or act in a way that wasn't in alignment with your values, beliefs, or love for Christ? What did you learn from that experience?

Nobody Wants to Die

Review the material on Caiaphas, the high priest, pointing out that he was not only a religious leader but also a political operator. He established a system that enabled the Jewish religious traditions to continue while turning the temple into an economic engine.

+ What did you learn about the temple economic system under Caiaphas's leadership? How did Jesus threaten this system?
+ What was Caiaphas's concern regarding Jesus? What was his intent?
+ Have someone reread Mark 14:60-64 and then Exodus 3:13-15 aloud. How did Jesus answer Caiaphas's question, and why did Caiaphas tear his clothes after hearing Jesus's response?
+ While Jesus is expressing the truth of who he is, what is Peter doing in the courtyard? If Peter had the courage to draw his sword in the garden and follow Jesus to Caiaphas's home, why do you think he caved when confronted in the courtyard?
+ How do we see self-preservation in the lives of Abraham, Isaac, and other biblical characters? What are some ways we practice self-preservation today? When have you observed or experienced a hesitancy to speak out, tell the truth, or take a stand?
+ Do you agree with the author that failing to challenge policies that harm marginalized communities not only enables harm but also makes us complicit in injustice? Why or why not?

Worth the Risk

+ How did slavery in the first-century Roman Empire differ from slavery in the eighteenth and nineteenth centuries in America? What thoughts, questions, and feelings arise in you when you think about slaves being used in the temple in Jesus's day?

♦ Why was it courageous for the slave girl of the high priest to speak with such boldness to Peter? How might she have been a gift of grace in Peter's life? What do you think of the possibility that, rather than trying to get Peter in trouble, she might have been pushing him to come to Jesus's aide? How might Jesus's views of slaves and women speak into that possibility?

♦ Why do you think we tend to reject the idea that opposition can be a force for good in our own lives?

Unlikely Opposition

Have someone read aloud again Mark 14:66-71.

♦ How do we see Peter deny Jesus *privately*, *publicly*, and then *explicitly* in these verses?

♦ In the other Gospel accounts of this story, the rooster crows once, but here in Mark's Gospel the rooster crows twice. Why do you think Peter didn't "wake up" after the rooster's first crow?

♦ The author suggests we all have our own "inconvenient roosters"—moments or reminders that shake us awake to what's right in front of us. What are some examples of inconvenient roosters that call us back to who we're meant to be as followers of Jesus? Share generally or personally, or both, as you are comfortable.

Point out that after the Resurrection, Jesus meets Peter by another fire, not for rebuke but for restoration. Have someone read aloud John 21:15-17.

♦ How do we see restoration in this scene? How does Jesus invite Peter back into the circle of belonging?

- After an experience of falling short, how have you experienced God's love calling you back for restoration and a renewed sense of calling?
- After reading and discussing the story of Peter's denial and restoration, what is your response to the following statement: *Everyone belongs to God, and we belong to each other.*

Optional Practice

Close the session by inviting participants to reflect on how God might be using unlikely opposition in their lives to refine them and open them to growth. Write the following in advance on a markerboard or chart paper. (Or create a handout to distribute.)

Prayerfully reflect on the following:

What unlikely opposition are you experiencing in your life right now? Here are a few examples (the possibilities are endless):

- Someone who constantly questions your decisions.
- Someone who never seems to understand you.
- Someone who challenges your beliefs.
- A situation that is causing you to question yourself.
- A situation that makes you feel insecure or uncertain.

Ask yourself:

- How is this person/situation refining me?
- What is this person/situation revealing about myself?
- How is this person/situation humbling me?
- What blind spots might this person/situation be revealing?

Allow time for participants to reflect and write. Then invite volunteers to share as they are comfortable. (Or you might break into small groups or pairs for sharing.)

Closing Prayer

God of holy interruptions and inconveniences, thank you for speaking to us through unexpected voices and unsettling moments. Soften our hearts so we may hear what is true. Give us courage to recognize the ways we turn away from you, and the grace to allow you to restore us with your love. May we be rooted in knowing that we belong to you and to one another. Amen.

Session 3
UNLIKELY FREEDOM
Barabbas

Session Objectives

This session's reading, reflection, discussion, and prayer will help participants:

+ explore the story of Jesus and Barabbas before Pilate through Jewish history and the dynamics between the Jewish people and the Roman Empire at play behind the scenes;
+ recognize that shame is a universal human experience, shaping our interactions, our fears, our silence, and our need to blame others;
+ consider the pervasive nature of shame, the ways it influences us and manifests in our lives, and the roots of shame that begin early in lives in our families of origin;
+ explore the idea of Jesus as a willing scapegoat and how this does or does not resonate with their understanding of atonement and grace; and

+ understand that just as Jesus didn't hold Barabbas's past against him, he doesn't hold ours against us; instead, he invites us to lay down shame and blame and walk in freedom.

Biblical Foundations

Now at the festival the governor was accustomed to release a prisoner for the crowd, anyone whom they wanted. At that time they had a notorious prisoner called Jesus Barabbas. So after they had gathered, Pilate said to them, "Whom do you want me to release for you, Jesus Barabbas or Jesus who is called the Messiah?" For he realized that it was out of jealousy that they had handed him over. While he was sitting on the judgment seat, his wife sent word to him, "Have nothing to do with that innocent man, for today I have suffered a great deal because of a dream about him." Now the chief priests and the elders persuaded the crowds to ask for Barabbas and to have Jesus killed. The governor again said to them, "Which of the two do you want me to release for you?" And they said, "Barabbas." Pilate said to them, "Then what should I do with Jesus who is called the Messiah?" All of them said, "Let him be crucified!" Then he asked, "Why, what evil has he done?" But they shouted all the more, "Let him be crucified!"

So when Pilate saw that he could do nothing but rather that a riot was beginning, he took some water and washed his hands before the crowd, saying, "I am innocent of this man's blood; see to it yourselves." Then the people as a whole answered, "His blood be on us and on our children!" So he released Barabbas for them, and after flogging Jesus he handed him over to be crucified.

Matthew 27:15-26

Now a man called Barabbas was in prison with the insurrectionists who had committed murder during the insurrection.

Mark 15:7

(This was a man who had been put in prison for an insurrection that had taken place in the city and for murder.)

Luke 23:19

The man said, "The woman whom you gave to be with me, she gave me fruit from the tree, and I ate." Then the LORD God said to the woman, "What is this that you have done?" The woman said, "The serpent tricked me, and I ate."

Genesis 3:12-13

Then Aaron shall lay both his hands on the head of the live goat and confess over it all the iniquities of the Israelites, and all their transgressions, all their sins, putting them on the head of the goat and sending it away into the wilderness by means of someone designated for the task. The goat shall bear on itself all their iniquities to a barren region, and the goat shall be set free in the wilderness.

Leviticus 16:21-22

Before Your Session

+ Carefully and prayerfully read this session's Biblical Foundations more than once. Note words and phrases that attract your attention and meditate on them. Write down questions you have and consult trusted Bible commentaries for further exploration if desired.
+ Carefully read chapter 3 of *An Unlikely Lent* by Rachel Billups.
+ You will need Bibles (or screen slides prepared with Scripture texts if meeting online; be sure to note the translation used); a markerboard or chart paper and markers; paper, pens or pencils; pieces of dissolvable paper and clear bowls of water.
+ If using the DVD or streaming video, preview the session 3 video segment.

Starting Your Session

Welcome participants and tell them that today we will be exploring our struggle with shame through the story of Jesus and Barabbas before Pilate. We will consider how our freedom from shame lies in our understanding of people like Barabbas, who offer us a glimpse of ourselves and our deep desire to fight for what is right and avoid shame at all costs, as well as our understanding of Jesus's unconditional love for us.

Share:

+ Tell the author's story about accidentally tearing a page in the family Bible and the shame she felt when her mother discovered what she had done—including how she lied about it.

Ask:

+ Why do you think we struggle with shame and try so hard to avoid it? (Invite participants to share brief responses.)

Opening Prayer

God, thank you for the opportunity today to explore a topic we tend to avoid: shame. As we study and discuss the moment when Jesus and Barabbas stood before Pilate, we ask you to open our hearts and minds to all that we can learn from this story. Deepen our faith in Christ and our sense of Christian community as we continue this Lenten journey together. Amen.

Video Presentation

Play the third track on the DVD or the streaming session of *An Unlikely Lent*, session 3 (running time is approximately 8–10 minutes). Discuss:

+ Which statements most interested, intrigued, surprised, or confused you? Why?
+ What new insights or questions does this video segment raise for you?

Book Discussion Questions

Shame, Shame

+ The author compares shame to a weighted blanket that wraps itself around you; you can still move, but you always feel its pressure crushing down on you. Does this description of shame resonate with you? Why or why not?
+ What were some of the spoken or unspoken messages about shame in your family of origin? Was shame ever used as a form of discipline or control, and if so, how did that affect you?
+ The author calls shame "the thing behind the thing." Are there any behaviors or reactions of yours that might be rooted in shame? Share as you are comfortable.
+ How have you seen shame lead to blame—in yourself or others? What would it look like to start naming shame instead of hiding or blaming? What kind of support would you need to do that?
+ Have someone read aloud Genesis 3:12-13. Does reframing the focus of this story as "original shame" rather than "original sin" shift your understanding of the story in any way?

We Need a Scapegoat

Briefly review the author's overview of the Maccabean Revolt of the second century BCE and the dynamics between the Jewish people and the Roman Empire at the time of Jesus. Then have a volunteer read aloud Matthew 27:15-18.

- What were the four Jewish sects and their respective strategies for survival under the iron grip of Rome? Which of these groups' responses do you most relate to—resisting through obedience, accommodation, withdrawal, or action?
- What do Matthew 27:16; Mark 15:7; and Luke 23:19 tell us about Jesus Barabbas? If it's true that he was not only a rebel against Rome but also a Zealot, as some scholars speculate, how would that make Pilate's question to the crowd a choice not only between two men but also between two visions of salvation? How do you see these two visions of salvation still at work in the world today?
- How could viewing Barabbas as a Zealot—someone who believes that resisting injustice is the only way to freedom— make Jesus a scapegoat for Barabbas's failure?
- Put yourself in Barabbas's shoes for a moment, expecting to die but suddenly being set free while someone else is condemned. How would it feel to be spared and have someone else take your place? What thoughts and feelings would you carry afterward?

Willing Scapegoat

- What do you think about the idea of Jesus as a *willing* scapegoat? Does this language resonate with your understanding of atonement and grace? Why or why not?
- What insights or questions does the discussion of the priestly rituals of purification—such as handwashing, the sprinkling of blood, and the use of a second goat—raise for you? In what ways does this symbolism deepen, complicate, or confuse your understanding of Jesus as the ultimate sacrifice?
- What does the crowd's choice of Barabbas reveal about human nature?

Read aloud the following excerpt:

> Matthew wanted us to see Jesus standing in for all of us. Barabbas went free, the crowd carried on, Pilate tried to wash off the guilt, but Jesus? He took it all. Substitutionary atonement is a part of Christian theology, this belief that Jesus did not just die, he died for us and instead of us....I wrestle with the theology of substitutionary atonement, not because I do not believe that atonement is important, but rather because Jesus's death seems bigger than a mere trade. Jesus's death seems more cosmic than just a one-for-one. Because what I know is that Jesus's life, death, and resurrection bring healing and restoration to all of God's broken creation.

+ Do you agree with the author that this story suggests Jesus's death was more than a one-for-one exchange? Why or why not? How do you understand the connection between Jesus's death on the cross and the restoration of all creation?

+ How would you explain the kind of justice Jesus invites us to embrace? What is the focus of this justice?

+ Brené Brown writes, "We're all afraid to talk about shame. The less we talk about shame, the more control it has over our lives." Have you experienced this to be true in your own life? How has shame influenced the way you carry blame, hide truth, or resist grace? How might naming your shame be a step toward healing and freedom?

Lose the Shame and Blame

+ Does the author's description of having a little kid inside her who just wants to get it right resonate with you? Why or why not? What messages about performance, perfection, and failure did you receive as a child or adolescent? How do those messages still surface in your life today?

+ What are some of the lies that shame tries to tell you? What truth do you need to speak to yourself when those voices get loud?

+ Jesus didn't hold Barabbas's past against him, and he doesn't hold our pasts against us. How might deeply internalizing this truth change the way you think about grace, forgiveness, and your own story? What would it look like for you to lay down shame and blame and believe you are defined by the love of the One who refuses to hold anything against you?

Optional Practice

Close the session by inviting participants to symbolically act out the truth that they are claimed, not shamed. Tell them that the weight of their past, the burden of guilt, the lies that whisper "not enough" do not have the final word; Jesus does! And Jesus's word is *freedom*.

In advance, set up clear bowls of water, representing the baptismal waters that claim us as God's beloved, and give each participant a piece of dissolvable paper. Instruct participants to write a word or phrase on the piece of paper representing a shame they've carried. It might be a mistake, a regret, or something spoken over them that made them believe they weren't worthy of love. Invite them to come forward when they're ready and place the paper in the water to dissolve.

Tell participants this is a sign and symbol that shame does not get to define them anymore. Just as the paper disappears, so does the power of shame when we release it into God's grace.

Invite participants to let their use of water throughout the coming week be a symbolic practice of remembrance. Whenever they are pouring a glass of water, washing their hands, taking a shower or bath, or using water in any way, they are to remember that their shame has been released into God's grace.

Closing Prayer

Gracious and loving God, you see the heavy loads we carry—burdens we were never meant to carry. Today and throughout the week, whenever we use water, remind us of the cleansing waters of baptism and what is most true: we are claimed, not shamed. We release what no longer serves us—every whisper of unworthiness, every lie we've believed. Wash us again in your mercy and grace. May we walk forward with unburdened hearts, knowing we are deeply loved, completely forgiven, and truly free—through Jesus Christ, our Savior and Companion on the journey. Amen.

Session 4
UNLIKELY COMPANIONSHIP
Simon of Cyrene

Session Objectives

This session's reading, reflection, discussion, and prayer will help participants:

+ consider the ways we try to avoid, numb, or distract ourselves from pain;

+ explore how suffering is more than pain to be avoided but a pathway to growth, life, and love and an invitation to let others walk with us;

+ recognize that we were designed to be in deep relationship with one another and that suffering can be an opportunity to share our pain and help carry one another's burdens;

- consider how Simon of Cyrene and the grieving women were unlikely companions to Jesus on his way to the cross, being present to his suffering;
- learn to offer presence rather than solutions when others are suffering; and
- view suffering not as punishment but as something sacred to share.

Biblical Foundations

As they led him away, they seized a man, Simon of Cyrene, who was coming from the country, and they laid the cross on him and made him carry it behind Jesus. A great number of the people followed him, and among them were women who were beating their breasts and wailing for him. But Jesus turned to them and said, "Daughters of Jerusalem, do not weep for me, but weep for yourselves and for your children. For the days are surely coming when they will say, 'Blessed are the barren, and the wombs that never bore, and the breasts that never nursed.' Then they will begin to say to the mountains, 'Fall on us,' and to the hills, 'Cover us.' For if they do this when the wood is green, what will happen when it is dry?"

Luke 23:26-31

And at this sound the crowd gathered and was bewildered, because each one heard them speaking in the native language of each. Amazed and astonished, they asked, "Are not all these who are speaking Galileans? And how is it that we hear, each of us, in our own native language? Parthians, Medes, Elamites, and residents of Mesopotamia, Judea and Cappadocia, Pontus and Asia, Phrygia and Pamphylia, Egypt and the parts of Libya belonging to Cyrene, and visitors from Rome, both Jews and proselytes, Cretans and Arabs—in our own languages we hear them speaking about God's deeds of power."

Acts 2:6-11

Before Your Session

+ Carefully and prayerfully read this session's Biblical Foundations more than once. Note words and phrases that attract your attention and meditate on them. Write down questions you have and consult trusted Bible commentaries for further exploration if desired.

+ Carefully read chapter 4 of *An Unlikely Lent* by Rachel Billups.

+ You will need Bibles (or screen slides prepared with Scripture texts if meeting online; be sure to note the translation used); a markerboard or chart paper and markers; paper, pens or pencils; battery-operated tea light candles (one for each group member).

+ If using the DVD or streaming video, preview the session 4 video segment.

Starting Your Session

Welcome participants and tell them that today we will be exploring how suffering is more than pain to be avoided; it's a pathway to growth, life, and love and an invitation to let others walk with us. We will consider how we were designed to be in deep relationship with one another and how suffering can be an opportunity to share our pain and help carry one another's burdens.

Share:

+ Our human tendency is to avoid and resist pain and suffering. We distract, numb, and pacify ourselves in many ways.

Ask:

+ What are your go-to methods for avoiding, resisting, or numbing pain—whether it's physical, emotional, or relational? (Invite participants to share brief responses.)

Opening Prayer

God, thank you for the opportunity today to address a universal reality of the human experience: suffering. As we study and discuss how others came alongside Jesus in his suffering on the way to the cross, we ask you to open our hearts and minds to all that we can learn from this part of the Passion story. Deepen our faith in Christ and our sense of Christian community as we continue this Lenten journey together. Amen.

Video Presentation

Play the fourth track on the DVD or the streaming session of *An Unlikely Lent*, session 4 (running time is approximately 8–10 minutes). Discuss:

+ Which statements most interested, intrigued, surprised, or confused you? Why?
+ What new insights or questions does this video segment raise for you?

Book Discussion Questions

I Didn't Sign Up for This

Talk briefly about how life seems to hand us moments that we did not willingly agree to experience. Most days we just want to embrace the good, go with what is comfortable, and avoid the conflict; but sometimes life hands us situations that we simply cannot ignore. That certainly was true for Simon of Cyrene. Have a volunteer read aloud Luke 23:26.

+ Have you ever experienced a moment when you thought "I didn't sign up for this"? What happened, and how did it shape or stretch you? Looking back, can you see any growth, change, or new perspective that emerged from that experience?

+ Simon of Cyrene was pulled into Jesus's suffering without warning. What do we know about him, and what is left to our imagination? What might his story teach us about the unexpected invitations that come to us? What can help us to discern whether a burden we didn't choose might also be a calling?

+ Our culture often encourages us to avoid suffering at all costs. At the beginning of our session, we shared some ways we try to avoid pain, whether it's physical, emotional, or relational. Do you believe it is ever helpful to avoid, numb, or distract ourselves from pain? If so, how can we discern when avoiding pain is helpful and when it is harmful? How can trying to avoid or numb pain sometimes keep us from growing or healing?

+ When and how have you seen suffering transformed into something creative, redemptive, or meaningful in your life or the lives of others?

Never Alone

Have a volunteer read aloud Luke 23:26-31.

+ Other than Simon of Cyrene, who were the other unexpected companions to Jesus in his suffering?

+ Simon and the women walked alongside Jesus in his pain, not to fix or remove it but simply to be present. How did the women demonstrate compassionate presence to Jesus?

+ What did Jesus say to the grieving women (see Luke 23:28-31)? How might we view this as an invitation to enter into his suffering?

+ The author writes, "We are not qualified to solve one another's problems most of the time, but we can simply be present." How can we learn to offer presence instead of solutions? What might this kind of presence look like in your relationships?

+ The author reflects on the tension between appearing strong and allowing ourselves to be supported. In what ways do you wrestle with this tension? What makes it difficult for you to let others see and meet your need?

+ In what ways have you been influenced by the cultural message that showing vulnerability means you are weak? The author writes, "Vulnerability is a doorway to connection." What helps and what hinders your ability to embrace vulnerability in community? How have you benefited from practicing vulnerability in community?

+ Father Gregory Boyle says, "We belong to one another, also no exceptions." In what ways does shared suffering reveal our interconnectedness? How might acknowledging our need for one another change the way we live, love, and serve?

Unlikely Companion

+ The author describes suffering as an "unlikely companion"—not something we seek, yet something we all experience. How has suffering been an "unlikely companion" to you or someone close to you, deepening your/their life and faith?

+ When sharing about her mother singing joyfully despite being close to death from pancreatic cancer, the author observes, "There is a divine mystery to this faith we hold so dear." When have you experienced or witnessed this divine mystery of genuine joy or peace being present in the midst of great pain?

+ The author writes, "We have a treasure in the church that we call lament." What does lament mean to you, and how is it different from simply complaining or venting? If lament is such a treasure, why do you think it is so neglected today? How comfortable are you with expressing anger, grief, or disappointment to God and to others?

♦ Simon of Cyrene didn't choose to carry Jesus's cross, yet he didn't refuse it. What might it look like for you to carry your own or someone else's pain not as something to escape, but as something sacred to share?

Optional Practice

Close the session by creating holy space for sharing in one another's suffering. Play soft music and place multiple battery-operated tea lights on a table at the front of the room. Then invite participants to come forward and light a candle as they reflect on and pray about their own suffering and pain or that of someone else. Remind them that the light is a sign that none of us suffers in isolation. As you witness the lights glowing together, acknowledge that you are not alone. Ask several people in advance to be prepared to pray with individuals if needed.

As you prepare to close in prayer, invite each participant to take one of the tea lights home and light it each day during the coming week as a spiritual practice, spending a few moments being mindful that they are not alone in their suffering.

Closing Prayer

Compassionate God, thank you for drawing near to us in our pain and suffering. And thank you for the gift of presence—for the ones who walk beside us, sometimes unexpectedly, offering quiet strength, comfort, and light. When the path seems dark, remind us that we are not alone. Help us rest in the truth that even then, love still holds. Amen

Session 5
UNLIKELY COURAGE
The Women at the Cross

Session Objectives

This session's reading, reflection, discussion, and prayer will help participants:

+ explore how the women at the cross show us what faithful discipleship looks like;
+ see these women not as extras in the Gospel story but as central figures of courage and devotion;
+ reflect on when and why they have been reluctant to step into a difficult or uncomfortable situation and when and why they, like the women at the cross, chose courage over comfort;
+ consider how Jesus created a new vision of family at the cross— one based not on blood but on love, faithfulness, and mutual care—and how the church is meant to be a true spiritual family to all persons; and

♦ explore the meaning of costly discipleship and the difference between being an admirer of Jesus and a disciple of Jesus.

Biblical Foundations

Many women were also there, looking on from a distance; they had followed Jesus from Galilee, ministering to him. Among them were Mary Magdalene, and Mary the mother of James and Joseph, and the mother of the sons of Zebedee.

Matthew 27:55-56

There were also women looking on from a distance. Among them were Mary Magdalene, and Mary the mother of James the younger and of Joses, and Salome, who followed him when he was in Galilee and ministered to him, and there were many other women who had come up with him to Jerusalem.

Mark 15:40-41

And when all the crowds who had gathered there for this spectacle saw what had taken place, they returned home, beating their breasts. But all his acquaintances, including the women who had followed him from Galilee, stood at a distance watching these things.

Luke 23:48-49

Meanwhile, standing near the cross of Jesus were his mother, and his mother's sister, Mary the wife of Clopas, and Mary Magdalene. When Jesus saw his mother and the disciple whom he loved standing beside her, he said to his mother, "Woman, here is your son." Then he said to the disciple, "Here is your mother." And from that hour the disciple took her into his own home.

John 19:25-27

Before Your Session

+ Carefully and prayerfully read this session's Biblical Foundations more than once. Note words and phrases that attract your attention and meditate on them. Write down questions you have and consult trusted Bible commentaries for further exploration if desired.
+ Carefully read chapter 5 of *An Unlikely Lent* by Rachel Billups.
+ You will need Bibles (or screen slides prepared with Scripture texts if meeting online; be sure to note the translation used); a markerboard or chart paper and markers; paper, pens or pencils; a flat wooden cross, hammer and nails, and index cards (or create a large cross out of bulletin board paper and use sticky notes).
+ If using the DVD or streaming video, preview the session 5 video segment.

Starting Your Session

Welcome participants and tell them that today we will be exploring how the women at the cross show us what faithful discipleship looks like. While the male disciples apparently fled in fear, these women stayed. Their courage stands as a challenge to us today.

Share:

+ We tend to crave comfort and cling to what feels safe and predictable.

Ask:

+ When have you felt torn between staying safe and stepping into a difficult or uncomfortable situation? (Invite participants to share brief responses.)

Opening Prayer

God, thank you for the opportunity today to explore what true discipleship looks like. As we study and discuss the courage of the women at the cross, we ask you to open our hearts and minds to all that we can learn from their example and their challenge to us. Deepen our faith in Christ and our sense of Christian community as we continue this Lenten journey together. Amen.

Video Presentation

Play the fifth track on the DVD or the streaming session of *An Unlikely Lent*, session 5 (running time is approximately 8–10 minutes). Discuss:

+ Which statements most interested, intrigued, surprised, or confused you? Why?
+ What new insights or questions does this video segment raise for you?

Book Discussion Questions

Craving Comfort

Have several volunteers read aloud the descriptions of the women at the cross from Matthew 27:55-56; Mark 15:40-41; and Luke 23:48-49.

+ How do the descriptions of the women at the cross differ in the Gospels of Matthew, Mark, and Luke? How does Luke "soften" the mention of the women in his account? The author offers some thoughts about why each of the Gospel writers might have recorded a different list of names for the women at the cross. What are your thoughts about this?

+ Why is it significant that Mark identifies Salome not for whose wife or mother she might have been but simply for who she was?

+ Each one of the Gospel writers mentions the women at the cross. In Luke 23:49 we read, "But all his acquaintances, including the women who *had followed* him from Galilee, stood at a distance watching these things" (emphasis added). The author points out that the use of "had followed" in reference to the women is language that signals discipleship. Does this information shift or deepen your understanding of the roles of these women? Why or why not? What might it mean for us as individuals and as the church to see these women not as extras in the Gospel narrative but as central figures of courage and devotion?

+ The author describes a brigade of faith-filled women who organize themselves and rally around folks in need. Have you ever witnessed or been part of such a community of women? In what ways have you *received* the quiet, faithful ministry of presence and care?

+ What are some examples of times when Jesus championed women, lifting them up and validating their dignity, honor, and worth? Given Jesus's treatment of women, why do you think people attempt to relegate women to the "religious sidelines"? Do you agree with the author that when we limit the role of women in the church, we limit the roles of everyone in the church? Why or why not?

+ Have you ever had an experience where someone attempted to limit *your* participation in the church? Perhaps it was because of where you grew up, your family of origin, your race, your primary language, or any other limiting factor. How can we help expand the vision of God's calling for *all* people?

+ When have you, like the women at the cross, stepped into a difficult or uncomfortable situation despite your unease or fear? What helped you choose courage over comfort?

Have a volunteer read aloud John 19:25-27. Acknowledge that it seems odd for John, "the beloved disciple," to be at the foot of the cross if the male disciples were in danger of being arrested. Then share scholar N. T. Wright's suggestion that John may have been very young, perhaps a teenager, and therefore not perceived as a threat.

+ If those at the foot of the cross were the ones society underestimated and overlooked—women and the young— what does this teach us about God's heart and how God works in the world? Who might we be overlooking in our churches or communities today?

A Different Kind of Faith

+ The author writes that the women's faith wasn't transactional but deeply personal. How would you explain what this means? How would you describe your own relationship with Jesus? What does it mean to you to stay with Jesus "no matter the cost"?
+ How did Jesus create a new vision of family at the cross—one based not on blood but on love, faithfulness, and commitment? How have you experienced the church as a true spiritual family? What commitments do we make to one another when we say yes to becoming a member of the body of Christ?
+ The author describes discipleship as "showing up"—bringing a casserole in crisis and advocating for the vulnerable. What does it look like in your life to "show up" in love for someone?
+ Clarence Jordan challenged his brother, saying, "You're an admirer of Jesus, not a disciple." How would you explain the

difference between admiring Jesus and following him? How does this stretch or challenge you?

+ The author writes, "The cost of following Jesus is not limited to what we say we believe. Following Jesus is about what we are willing to lose." What are you being asked to risk or let go of for the sake of Jesus and others?

Courageously Follow Jesus

+ What stands out to you most about the women who stayed at the cross? How was their presence at the cross an act of defiance against fear? What might defiant love and faithful presence look like in your own life right now?

+ These women followed Jesus without knowing the outcome. How does uncertainty impact your ability to trust and follow Jesus?

+ Are there areas in your faith where you tend to admire Jesus from a distance rather than follow him closely—especially when it's hard? What might it look like to move closer?

+ The author writes, "The cross demands an answer." How would you explain what this means? What does courageous, costly discipleship look like in your life, your church, and your community?

Optional Practice

Close the session by playing some worship music and inviting participants to express their "answer to the cross" with a symbolic action. Begin by saying that when we look at the world and whisper, "Someone should do something about that," perhaps Jesus is whispering back, "Yes, you." That gentle nudge is the Spirit calling us to step in. Following Jesus means we stop waiting for others to fix what's broken and, instead, partner with God to take up the work of restoration.

Have each participant write on an index card (or sticky note) the burden that is stirring in their heart—the injustice, the pain, the need they can no longer ignore. Then invite them to come forward one at a time to nail the card to a wooden cross (or attach the sticky note to a paper cross). Tell them that this is not about guilting anyone into action; this is about receiving God's grace. With this action they are saying, "Jesus, I will go where you go. I will follow, even when it is hard, even when it costs me." Reassure participants that this act does not mean they will have all the answers or even all the courage they need. It means they are committing to start. Sometimes the most powerful faith begins when we simply say, "I'm willing."

As you prepare to close in prayer, invite participants to pray about their commitment throughout the week and listen for God's guidance regarding their first (or next) right step.

Closing Prayer

Jesus, you know how much we long for comfort and certainty—especially when life feels uncertain and hard. Yet you call us to a deeper path, one that may cost us but never leaves us alone. Strengthen our hearts as you did for the women at the cross. Give us the courage to follow you even when it's difficult and help us encourage one another along the way. Remind us that we don't walk this road alone—we walk it together, held by your love. Amen.

Session 6
UNLIKELY ALLIES
Joseph of Arimathea
and Nicodemus

Session Objectives

This session's reading, reflection, discussion, and prayer will help participants:

+ explore how Joseph of Arimathea and Nicodemus show us what it means to step out of safety into courageous faith;

+ view these men's bold action as an act of surrender, courage, and a public declaration that "Jesus is King and Lord";

+ understand the ministry of presence and why it is so powerful;

+ recognize that God moves us to join in God's work of justice in the world, and that God does not send us alone but forms unlikely allies in the most unlikely of places; and

+ consider how God may be calling them to step up as an unlikely ally in a world that desperately needs healing and hope.

Biblical Foundations

Since it was the day of Preparation, the Jews did not want the bodies left on the cross during the Sabbath, especially because that Sabbath was a day of great solemnity. So they asked Pilate to have the legs of the crucified men broken and the bodies removed. Then the soldiers came and broke the legs of the first and of the other who had been crucified with him. But when they came to Jesus and saw that he was already dead, they did not break his legs. Instead, one of the soldiers pierced his side with a spear, and at once blood and water came out. (He who saw this has testified so that you also may believe. His testimony is true, and he knows that he tells the truth, so that you also may continue to believe.) These things occurred so that the scripture might be fulfilled, "None of his bones shall be broken." And again another passage of scripture says, "They will look on the one whom they have pierced."

After these things, Joseph of Arimathea, who was a disciple of Jesus, though a secret one because of his fear of the Jews, asked Pilate to let him take away the body of Jesus. Pilate gave him permission, so he came and removed his body. Nicodemus, who had at first come to Jesus by night, also came, bringing a mixture of myrrh and aloes, weighing about a hundred pounds. They took the body of Jesus and wrapped it with the spices in linen cloths, according to the burial custom of the Jews. Now there was a garden in the place where he was crucified, and in the garden there was a new tomb in which no one had ever been laid. And so, because it was the Jewish day of Preparation and the tomb was nearby, they laid Jesus there.

John 19:31-42

Now there was a Pharisee named Nicodemus, a leader of the Jews. He came to Jesus by night and said to him, "Rabbi, we know that you are a teacher who has come from God, for no one can do these signs that you do unless God is with that person."

John 3:1-2

Before Your Session

+ Carefully and prayerfully read this session's Biblical Foundations more than once. Note words and phrases that attract your attention and meditate on them. Write down questions you have and consult trusted Bible commentaries for further exploration if desired.

+ Carefully read chapter 6 of *An Unlikely Lent* by Rachel Billups.

+ You will need Bibles (or screen slides prepared with Scripture texts if meeting online; be sure to note the translation used); a markerboard or chart paper and markers; paper, pens or pencils; music, candles, and other desired elements for creating a sacred space; small, smooth stones and permanent markers; bowl, basket, or another container.

+ If using the DVD or streaming video, preview the session 6 video segment.

Starting Your Session

Welcome participants and tell them that today we will be exploring how Joseph of Arimathea and Nicodemus show us what it means to step out of safety into courageous faith. Their bold action was an act of surrender, courage, and a public declaration that "Jesus is King and Lord." They also show us that God does not send us alone but forms unlikely allies in the most unlikely of places.

Share:

+ God works in our hearts, moving us to join in God's work of justice in the world by loving our neighbors in tangible ways, often forming very unlikely relationships.

Ask:

+ When have you sensed God working in your heart in this way, moving you to take bold action and perhaps form unlikely relationships for love of neighbor and justice in the world?

Opening Prayer

God, thank you for the opportunity today to explore God's call to act boldly and risk unlikely relationships for the sake of your kingdom work. As we study and discuss the courageous acts of Joseph of Arimathea and Nicodemus, we ask you to open our hearts and minds to all that we can learn from their example. Deepen our faith in Christ and our sense of Christian community as we conclude our Lenten journey together. Amen.

Video Presentation

Play the sixth track on the DVD or the streaming session of *An Unlikely Lent*, session 6 (running time is approximately 8–10 minutes). Discuss:

+ Which statements most interested, intrigued, surprised, or confused you? Why?
+ What new insights or questions does this video segment raise for you?

Book Discussion Questions

Unlikely Relationships

Share the story of Daryl Davis in your own words. Then read this excerpt from *An Unlikely Lent*:

Could it be that love—real inside-out, take-the-first-step kind of love—has the power to transform enemies into friends, rivals into partners, and strangers into allies? Could it be that the people we are most likely to dismiss, the ones we assume are just "not our people," are the very ones God is calling us to know? When we engage in calm conversation, when we listen well and love regardless, something miraculous happens. We stop seeing each other as adversaries. We start seeing each other as human beings. In that work of reconciliation, we might just discover an unlikely ally.

+ How does Davis's courage and willingness to step into conversations and then unlikely friendships with adversaries challenge your faith?

+ Have you ever experienced an unlikely friendship—one that began in misunderstanding, rivalry, or even conflict? What changed the dynamic? What helped to build trust?

+ Why do you think it's so difficult today to believe that real transformation can happen through calm conversation and compassionate presence? How might Jesus be inviting us to resist division in our daily lives?

+ Is there someone in your life you tend to dismiss or avoid? If so, what might it look like to take a small step toward connection, understanding, or perhaps even reconciliation?

Everyday Obligations

Have a volunteer read aloud John 19:31-42. Say that Joseph of Arimathea and Nicodemus were members of the Sanhedrin, religious leaders who played vital roles in the community and carried a lot of responsibility.

- What kind of pressure do you imagine these men must have felt? What daily pressures and obligations are weighing heavily on *you*—whether at home, at work, or in the community?

- Why do you think Joseph of Arimathea was a secret disciple and Nicodemus approached Jesus under the cover of night (see John 3:1-2)?

- In what ways are we, like Joseph and Nicodemus, "cautiously curious"—desiring to follow Jesus and be an authentic disciple yet struggling to assimilate our faith through all of life's obligations, challenges, and potential risks? Share generally or from your own experience as you are comfortable.

- We do not know whether Nicodemus and Joseph were at the trial of Jesus, remaining quiet to preserve their power, or heard of it later, realizing their protests were too late. Either way, they showed up at the cross despite the fact that they were not model followers of Jesus. How does their public act of love and courage move you? How does their example challenge you in your own faith journey?

Ministry of Presence

- We talked about the power of presence in sessions 4 and 5. Here in chapter 6 of *An Unlikely Lent* the author uses the term "ministry of presence." What does this mean to you, and why do you think the ministry of presence is so powerful, especially in seasons of grief or suffering?

Read aloud this excerpt from *My Parting Prescription for America* written by former US Surgeon General Dr. Vivek Murthy:

The love required to build community must not be reserved only for close family and friends or those who share our beliefs and life experiences; it must also be extended to neighbors, colleagues, people of different backgrounds, people with whom we disagree, and even people we consider our opponents. It requires recognizing something deeper and more fundamental that connects us.

+ How would you describe the kind of love that builds community with those who do not think, believe, or live like us? What makes that kind of love difficult—and what makes it transformative? Who in your life might God be inviting you to love more deeply or differently?

+ According to John 19:39, what did Nicodemus bring? How does the weight of the spices help us to interpret Nicodemus's actions? What kind of declaration might he and Joseph have been making?

Unlikely You

+ Joseph and Nicodemus didn't make public confessions of faith in Jesus, but they eventually showed up, spoke up, and stood up on his behalf—asking for his body, preparing it for burial, and placing it in a tomb. What does this teach us about how God calls the most unlikely people to stand in the gap for those who cannot speak or act for themselves?

+ The author shares several stories of unlikely leaders who took small actions that grew into movements. Which story stands out to you most, and why?

+ The world still needs people who will "stand where others step aside, speak when silence is easy, and love when hate feels inevitable." Where do you see this kind of need right now? How might you begin a hard conversation where reconciliation is needed in your family, your church, or your community?

+ What holds you back from stepping into the role of an "unlikely ally"? What might help you take one small step of courage?

Optional Practice

Close the session by creating a quiet and reflective environment—perhaps with soft music and candles. Distribute smooth stones and permanent markers to each person. Invite participants to prayerfully consider how God may be calling them to step up as an unlikely ally in a world that desperately needs healing and hope. Offer the following prompts (you also may want to write them on a markerboard or chart paper in advance):

+ Is there an injustice you've noticed—in your neighborhood, your city, or the wider world—that stirs your heart?
+ Is God nudging you to be a listening ear, a healing presence, or a bridge between divided people?
+ Are you sensing a shift from cautious curiosity to courageous commitment in your own faith journey?
+ Is there a specific way God is calling you to embody the ministry of presence?

Encourage participants to write a word, phrase, or short commitment on the stone—something that symbolizes how they feel led to respond. This could be as simple as "Be Present," "Speak Up," or "Pray Boldly." Once everyone has had time to reflect and write, invite them to bring their stone forward and place it in a communal bowl, basket, or on a central table—creating a visual altar of commitment. Let them know that this sacred gesture mirrors the courage of Joseph of Arimathea and Nicodemus—men who stepped forward in an unlikely way and at great personal risk to honor Jesus.

You might say something like this:

By placing your stone here, you are saying, "Jesus is my King and my Lord." This is an expression of courage and a declaration of hope. Know that you are not alone. God goes with you—and will send others to walk beside you in unexpected ways. You are part of something bigger—a kingdom movement of unlikely allies.

After the closing prayer, invite participants to take their stone home and keep it as a tangible reminder of their commitment—placing it somewhere they will see it often as a prompt for prayer and action.

Closing Prayer

Gracious and surprising God, you often work through the unlikely—people like Joseph of Arimathea and Nicodemus, and people like us. We confess how easy it is to hold back and stay in the safety of cautious faith. Yet you continue to whisper courage into our hearts. Keep stirring within us, shaping not only our intentions but also the rhythms of our days. Show us where love needs to take on flesh in our neighborhoods, our relationships, and our communities. Make your invitations unmistakable—where we're called to make peace, to take a stand, or to join your healing work in the world. Give us grace to respond with boldness, knowing we never walk alone. Amen.

Watch videos based on *An Unlikely Lent* with Rachel Billups through Amplify Media.

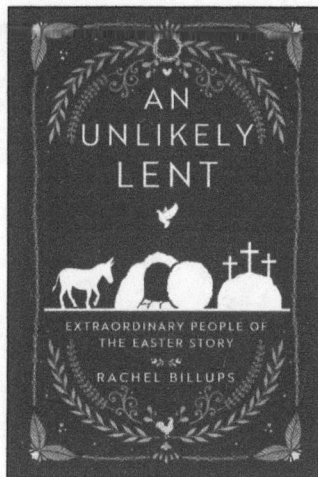

Amplify Media is a multimedia platform that delivers high-quality, searchable content with an emphasis on Wesleyan perspectives for churchwide, group, or individual use on any device at any time. In a world of sometimes overwhelming choices, Amplify gives church leaders and congregants media capabilities that are contemporary, relevant, effective and, most important, affordable and sustainable.

With *Amplify Media* church leaders can:

+ Provide a reliable source of Christian content through a Wesleyan lens for teaching, training, and inspiration in a customizable library
+ Deliver their own preaching and worship content in a way the congregation knows and appreciates
+ Build the church's capacity to innovate with engaging content and accessible technology
+ Equip the congregation to better understand the Bible and its application
+ Deepen discipleship beyond the church walls

⋀ AMPLIFY MEDIA

Ask your group leader or pastor about Amplify Media and sign up today at www.AmplifyMedia.com.

www.ingramcontent.com/pod-product-compliance
Lightning Source LLC
Chambersburg PA
CBHW022111240226
40163CB00007B/21